Believe in
Yourself
and
Do What
You Love

KATE JAMES

Andrews McMeel
PUBLISHING®

Praise for Kate James and Total Balance

"I absolutely adore Kate. She is a highly skilled, generous, and enormously gifted business coach, especially for those who don't traditionally consider themselves 'business people.'"
— *Clare Bowditch, Big Hearted Business*

"Kate really 'walks the talk' and is clearly someone who has a great deal of expertise to share. Thank you, Kate!"
— *Robert Gerrish, Flying Solo*

"Kate James is a generous, creative coach who is passionate about helping others fulfill their dreams and brilliant at helping people move through both inner and outer obstacles."
— *Elise Bialylew, Founder of Mindful in May*

"I would not hesitate to recommend Kate James of Total Balance to anyone who has goals and dreams, be it for life or business, that they want to achieve and don't know where to begin, or how to get there."
— *Jodie Holmes, Director of Seaside Creative*

"Put simply, working with Kate helped me to get clear—which has been nothing short of life changing."
— *Leanne Clancey, Food & Travel Writer*

Contents

Introduction

When I was twenty, I had no idea what I wanted to do with my life.

I was still confused at thirty. Mostly, I made choices that were about pleasing other people and looking good to the outside world. It wasn't until my passionate and independent grandmother died in my mid-thirties that it suddenly dawned on me: life is short and I should do what matters to me most. I threw in my marketing degree and started my own business.

I wanted to spend my days helping people, but I didn't know if I could build a business from the ground up—believing in myself came later.

Within this book, you'll find a collection of the things that helped me most. There are tips and exercises to develop your self-belief, and ideas about how to connect with the creative, inspired version of yourself so that you feel ready to start doing the things you love.

Read the book from cover to cover or flick through it at random. You might find just what you need. Carry it around with you for a month and dip in and out of it when you need a reminder that it's really not that hard to do things differently.

YOU JUST NEED TO MAKE A START—
LIKE I DID. IT WAS THE BEST
DECISION I EVER MADE.

Kati

1. How happy are you?

Are you happy with your life?

Answer yes or no to the following questions, then add up how many statements apply to you to see how satisfied you are with the life you are currently living.

I know my strengths and natural talents and how I can use them.

_____

I have a "bigger picture" purpose in life and know how I will achieve this.

_____

I value creativity and make time to pursue creative interests (even though I may not be a musician or an artist).

_____

I have a clear picture of three important things I would like to achieve in the next twelve months, and I know how I will reach these goals.

_____

I have defined my own version of success.

_____

I know how to keep myself motivated with regard to achieving my goals.

_____

I feel a sense of control over my finances and financial plans.

I love my work and feel that what I do is aligned with my values.

I feel free to communicate in an open and honest way in all of my important relationships.

Others find me inspiring and positive because of the way I live my life.

I know how to say no when I need to.

I make time on a regular basis for my personal development.

I have a supportive network of friends who encourage me to live in accordance with my values.

I feel confident to be myself.

I know how I self-sabotage and I make a conscious effort to overcome those habits.

I have at least one interest or hobby of my own.

How happy are you?

I eat a healthy diet,
manage alcohol and coffee
intake, and exercise at
least three times per week.

I make time to do
something indulgent or
relaxing for myself
every week.

I take annual vacations and
really unwind.

I feel calm and in control
most of the time.

/20

If your score is 15 or over, you're happier than most people! Give this book to someone who needs it more.

Anywhere between 10 and 15, you're doing okay, but you could do with some positive change. Flick through the book for ideas.

> THE MOST IMPORTANT THING IS GETTING STARTED, SO MAKE SURE YOU COMPLETE ONE ACTION STEP THIS WEEK.

If it's 10 or below, you might benefit from some support as well as trying the tips included here.

2. Be mindful

Before you can truly start believing in yourself and doing what you love, you need to become aware of how you're not believing in yourself and doing what you love right now. You can do that simply by becoming more mindful.

Being mindful means paying attention to what you're thinking, saying, and doing. It sounds easy, doesn't it? But you'd be amazed at how absentminded we become in modern life. We tend to think of the *next* thing, the *last* thing, the *worst* thing, anything but the thing we're actually supposed to be engaged with at that very moment.

When you create the headspace to step back and look at your life in a mindful way, you'll often discover a different perspective and become better able to identify the things that matter.

MINDFUL PEOPLE HAVE THE CAPACITY TO LOOK AT THEIR LIVES OBJECTIVELY.

They know how to keep their emotions in check, they don't judge themselves too harshly, and they can make wise, practical choices about how to move forward—particularly when life doesn't go to plan.

Be mindful

Learning to be mindful begins with slowing down to pay attention to what's happening in the given moment. Start here.

Drink a glass of water and think to yourself, "I am drinking a glass of water." Now you're being mindful.

Just be aware of what you're doing at any given moment. Ask yourself what you're doing throughout the day if that helps. "I am writing an email"/"I am waiting for a friend"/"I am at the bar"/"I am walking in nature"/"I am eating a sandwich"/"I am putting my child's seatbelt on."

You might set yourself little reminders like these to slow down and be in the moment. And when you are in the moment, ask yourself:

"What matters most to me at this point in my life?"

3. Everyone is creative

Give a four-year-old a box of crayons and a sheet of paper and he'll happily draw his family, house, garden (and a dog or cat, even if he doesn't have one).

Without a well-developed inner critic, he has a fundamental capacity for imagination and creativity.

Ask the same of a twelve-year-old and if he feels he has innate talent, he'll complete the task with confidence, but if not he'll most likely resist the offer.

Unless you've participated in creative activity in your adult life, you probably shy away from it too. Maybe you tell yourself you're not naturally creative.

Everyone is creative

Creativity is inherent in all of us, and even though we know that a person doesn't need to look like a person for a painting to be classified as great art, most of us have an irrational fear of getting it wrong. So we don't participate.

Being creative is not just about being able to create art; it's as much about being open-minded and having the capacity to think up new ideas or link information in different ways. It's having the ability to find novel solutions to problems, and we're all capable of that.

BEING CREATIVE LOWERS YOUR STRESS LEVELS, HELPS DECREASE NEGATIVE EMOTIONS, AND GENERALLY IMPROVES WELL-BEING.

That's according to many reports, including one from *The American Journal of Public Health* in 2010.

Try these ideas to help you to connect with the innovative, artistic part of you.

Make time to daydream. Research says that allowing your mind to wander helps to boost creative thinking.

———————————

Listen to a different style of music or see a play or a film you wouldn't normally see. Better still, take a music lesson, join an improv group, or make a short film of your own.

———————————

Try a new recipe, but not just any recipe. Choose a cuisine you've never cooked before and use a handful of ingredients you're not familiar with.

———————————

Be a tourist in your own city for a day. Visit somewhere new, take photographs, and immerse yourself in the experience like you would when you're traveling.

———————————

Set aside fifteen minutes every day to do something creative. Sketch, paint, play music, take photos, write poetry, or update a journal.

———————————

4. It's okay to be vulnerable

There's a paradox in learning to believe in yourself.

You need to be comfortable with the fact that being human means you're not going to be great at everything. That thought leaves most of us feeling a bit vulnerable.

We all bluff our way through situations to avoid embarrassment, and we probably became quite adept at concealing our weaknesses from others when we were teenagers. While it may seem counterintuitive, as we mature and get more comfortable in our own skin, it becomes easier to allow yourself to be vulnerable—to be the person who says, "Actually, I'm not sure,"—than it is to pretend.

Being vulnerable builds trust in relationships, it gives you room to grow, and it provides the opportunity for you to ask for help as you move toward your dreams.

People are drawn to authenticity, and being willing to own your weaknesses (as well as your strengths) means you can just be yourself.

Once you know your weak points, consider whether they are critical factors to your success. If you believe that you can't be successful without those traits, get some support to develop them. Otherwise find someone who has these qualities as their strengths and engage them to work with you.

But first, stop pretending. Drop your guard and be real.

> What makes you vulnerable
> makes you beautiful.
>
> — Brené Brown

5. Discover your strengths

Research (and common sense) says that when people spend their days doing things that they're naturally good at, they're more likely to feel engaged and happy.

Try the following exercises to discover your natural strengths.

1. WRITE DOWN EVERYTHING YOU LOVE DOING.

Include personal stuff, work stuff, and any random skills that come naturally to you. If you're stuck, think about the times when the hours pass quickly or when an activity feels effortless. You won't necessarily feel deliriously happy when you're using your strengths, but you will feel absorbed and engaged.

- You love chatting to friends about their travel plans, relationship issues, or a new business idea. *Your strengths could be listening, relationship building, curiosity, or helping others.*

- You love spending a Saturday reorganizing a room or thrifting for a new outfit. *Your strengths could be creativity, appreciation of beauty, or attention to detail.*

- You love learning about complex ideas and sharing what you've learned with others. *Your strengths could be love of learning, perspective, strategic thinking, or storytelling.*

- You love meeting new people and putting others in touch with one another when they might be able to mutually benefit. *Your strengths could be social intelligence, networking, curiosity, or making a difference.*

- You love brainstorming solutions to business problems and creating links between seemingly unrelated concepts. *Your strengths could be creativity, problem-solving, or decision-making.*

Discover your strengths

2. ASK YOUR FRIENDS AND FAMILY.

Shoot an email to ten friends and/or family members and ask them to identify at least five words that come to mind when they think about your natural strengths.

3. TAKE A SURVEY.

Try the free VIA Signature Strengths survey from the Positive Psychology team—www.viacharacter.org.

6. Develop unrealized strengths

Most of us favor certain strengths and get comfortable using and relying on those. As well as knowing and using your innate strengths, you also need to understand the difference between unrealized strengths and weaknesses.

Unrealized strengths are areas you may have a small amount of talent in but you're not confident enough to claim the strength as your own. It might be an area you feel somewhat drawn to—even if you're not sure why—and generally, the idea of exploring the strength further (even if it scares you), excites you a little, too.

Develop unrealized strengths

Weaknesses, on the other hand, are the things that drain you. They make you feel tired, depleted, or disconnected from what you're doing. You're better off to avoid them whenever you can.

Look at the list on the next page and think about areas you'd be interested in developing in order to realize your full potential. Don't be afraid to push yourself out of your comfort zone.

ONCE YOU'VE NOMINATED THE STRENGTHS YOU WANT TO WORK ON, WRITE DOWN SPECIFIC ACTIONS THAT WILL HELP YOU BRING THOSE STRENGTHS TO LIFE IN THE COMING WEEKS.

This is something you can continue to do for a lifetime—it's one of the fundamental principles of personal development.

While you're at it, you might want to put a cross next to any weaknesses so you can remember to keep away from these as much as possible.

For example, to grow these strengths:

PERSISTENCE: Push through the excuses you've been making in one area of your life. Set yourself a goal that stretches you and stick with it.

EMPATHY: Think about someone whose life is more difficult than yours. Do something thoughtful—make a call, offer a hand, volunteer, cook a meal, or just be there to listen.

STRATEGY: Step it up at work without being asked. Ask your boss about the big-picture view for your department or your organization and offer your opinion, even at the risk of being wrong.

COURAGE: For the next month, do one thing each week that takes you out of your comfort zone. Courage is like a muscle; in order to develop it you need to flex it regularly.

OPTIMISM: If your natural inclination is toward "glass half empty" thinking, spend a few complaint-free days and proactively start looking for things to be positive about.

What are your strengths?

Being persuasive	Authenticity
Curiosity	Confidence
Innovation	Self-awareness
Storytelling	Optimism
Getting things done	Listening
Spirituality	Explaining
Building esteem	Helping
Persistence	Writing
Attention to details	Performing

Making a
contribution to
society

Building
relationships

Decisiveness

Planning

Seeking adventure

Organizing

Judgment

Improving

Courage

Empathy

Kindness

Humility

Gratitude

Networking

Leading

Focus

7. Understand your purpose

Most of us want to make a difference in some way. What is one impact you'd like to make in the world? One thing you'd like to be remembered for?

You don't need to save starving children in Africa to be doing something meaningful, but you do need to understand *why you want to do what you do.*

People who know their purpose (the reason they're doing what they're doing) feel more deeply connected to their goals. They can usually tell their story in a more compelling way and they find it easier to get others on board to help them.

SOME EXAMPLES OF OTHER PEOPLE'S LIFE PURPOSE:

To be an advocate for those who are disadvantaged in some way.

To create a loving, nurturing family.

To make others feel great about themselves.

To bring humor and lightness into other people's lives.

To live an unconventional life and to inspire others to do the same.

To help people grow by fostering a love of learning.

To design objects that bring beauty into people's lives.

To share ideas that challenge traditional ways of thinking.

To live a spiritual life and to be a role model for others.

To educate underprivileged children so that they break free from a cycle of poverty.

To inspire people to live more sustainable, environmentally aware lives.

WHAT ABOUT YOU?
WHAT'S YOUR PURPOSE?

Steve Pavlina developed this exercise on his blog, *Personal Development for Smart People,* to help people connect with their life purpose.

Give yourself half an hour and a blank page.

Write, "My purpose is . . ." and then add whatever comes to mind beneath it. Keep writing, beginning each new line in the same way. Keep going until you feel moved or inspired—once you get to the point of feeling some emotion, you're pretty close to finding your purpose.

My purpose is . . .

8. Who are you trying to please?

We're hardwired for connection, so naturally we are inclined to want to please other people.

In ancient times, survival depended on being part of a pack. So well before it was social suicide to wear the wrong outfit to a party, it was literally a death sentence if you chose not to run with the crowd.

But there comes a point in everyone's life when you stop making decisions to please other people, and start making decisions that will make you happy. Think hard about the decisions you make. Are they helping to build your self-belief, or are they making you feel like an imposter?

We all feel a deep need to please, belong, and be safe and secure. But then we risk becoming conditioned to resisting change and avoiding risk.

Who are you trying to please?

When we're not being true to ourselves, we become increasingly uneasy, and try to cure that uneasiness with *stuff*. A few drinks, a new job, an old lover, a splurge on the credit card, designer shoes, a new European car . . . whatever it will take to quiet that nagging voice, the one that's asking, *"Who are you and what do you really want?"*

> SOME OF US ARE VAGUE
> VERSIONS OF OURSELVES,
> BUT THE REAL AND AUTHENTIC
> "YOU" NEVER GOES AWAY.

There might be one or two people you genuinely care about pleasing—your partner, a good friend, your children—but if you find yourself being agreeable with everyone, it's time to start being real.

Catch yourself when you're in "pleasing people" mode and learn to get comfortable with criticism. No matter what you do in your life, some people won't agree with your choices.

Set your own path. Get to know your values, your unique strengths, and your passions. Keep moving in the direction of your dreams, regardless of what other people think.

Be kind to yourself along the way and learn to speak to yourself like you'd speak to a best friend.

Take your foot off the pedal when you're feeling exhausted and practice self-care to keep your energy levels up.

Go easy on yourself when you make a mistake or change your mind. You don't need to do it all perfectly. Remind yourself that it takes courage to create any kind of change and it doesn't matter if you get it wrong sometimes.

Remember that sometimes you need to stand your ground and disagree with someone.

Celebrate small successes along the way.

9. Meditate on it

One of the best ways to become more self-aware is to practice meditation on a regular basis.

Meditation doesn't have to be about wearing hemp and sitting under a tree with your legs crossed chanting "ohm." In recent years, meditation has become mainstream. It's practiced by doctors, bankers, lawyers, and IT gurus as well as creative and spiritual types. To be honest, so many people get a boost from meditation these days that you're probably at a disadvantage if you don't meditate.

MEDITATION IS AN ANTIDOTE TO THE
BUSYNESS THAT CHARACTERIZES MOST
OF OUR LIVES, AND IT'S OFTEN THE
ONLY TIME WE FULLY SWITCH OFF.
THE BENEFITS ARE ASTOUNDING.

The science says that meditation is not just great for keeping
you calm—it thickens the brain tissue in the areas associated
with memory, decision-making, learning, and perspective-
taking. So it makes you smarter and improves your
performance. It will also help you sleep better and you'll be
more creative, calm, and focused—as well as more mindful
and aware.

Try it for yourself

Find a quiet space where you won't be interrupted for five minutes, and flick your phone onto silent.

Now, close your eyes and take a few deep breaths. Make sure you take your breath right down into your belly and make your outward breath really long and slow. Try to focus your full attention on breathing. You'll notice thoughts pop into your head (the first one will probably be "I wonder if I'm doing this right"). Do your best not to get caught up in your thoughts but equally, don't fight with them or try not to have thoughts. When you've noticed your mind has wandered away from the breath, just guide it back gently. At the end of what you think might be five minutes, open your eyes and sit for a minute or two before getting up. That's all it takes to meditate. You might not feel like you can go and conquer the world right now, but spend five to ten minutes doing just that every day (or every other day) and you'll soon feel the benefit.

10. What are your values?

It's easy to be seduced by what the media tells us makes a successful life, but ultimately you need to decide for yourself and not have values projected onto your life by others.

Values are the beliefs and ideals you consider important. Think of them as the benchmarks by which you can measure whether your life is being "well-lived." No values are better than others and our values can change across a lifetime—at every point in time you need to know your most important values so you can make mindful choices that align with them.

Sometimes our values can seem paradoxical—even if fame, fortune, and power are the things that matter most to you, you still might well find that living a life of security, integrity, and kindness is what will make you feel truly fulfilled.

What are your values?

Choose the ten values that matter most to you today. If there's something important that's not included in this list, add it in. Once you've chosen your values, put a score next to each of them as to how aligned you are with that value at this point in time; 10 being "completely aligned" and 1 being "not at all."

Keep in mind that most people find it impossible to live in perfect alignment with every one of their values at any given point in time.

LOOK AT THE SCORES THAT RATE LOW. WHAT'S ONE THING YOU CAN DO THIS WEEK THAT WILL PUT YOU IN GREATER SYNC WITH THE WAY YOU WANT TO LIVE?

- [ ] Family happiness
- [ ] Self-respect
- [ ] Generosity
- [ ] Competitiveness
- [ ] Recognition
- [ ] Wisdom
- [ ] Friendship
- [ ] Status
- [ ] Spirituality
- [ ] Affection
- [ ] Health
- [ ] Loyalty
- [ ] Teamwork
- [ ] Responsibility
- [ ] Culture
- [ ] Adventure
- [ ] Inner harmony
- [ ] Fame

- [ ] Achievement
- [ ] Involvement
- [ ] Order
- [ ] Wealth
- [ ] Economic security
- [ ] Creativity
- [ ] Connection
- [ ] Pleasure
- [ ] Integrity
- [ ] Freedom
- [ ] Power
- [ ] Personal development
- [ ] Sense of purpose and meaning
- [ ] Aesthetic appreciation
- [ ] Sustainability
- [ ] Contribution to society

11. What do you love?

Doing what you love is energizing and it makes you happy.

Create a list of everything you love doing. Don't worry about whether the things on your list will seem interesting or impressive to others—just think about anything that matters to you. Don't concern yourself with whether you're particularly gifted in a given area—just think of the activities that leave you feeling absorbed and engaged.

MAKE TIME FOR THE
THINGS YOU LOVE

Do you love . . . ?

Photography	Fashion	Reading
Acting	Numbers	Socializing
Writing	Illustrating	Gardening
Playing guitar	Food	Technology
Surfing	Interior design	Volunteering
Music	Politics	Minimalism
Fine art	Camping	Travel
Cooking	Bicycles	Nature
Singing	Craft	Spirituality

What do you love?

Work, relationships, exercise, shopping, cooking, sleeping, and mundane things like tidying the house can often get in the way of doing what you love.

DON'T WAIT UNTIL YOU CAN FIND THE TIME OR HAVE SPARE TIME, YOU NEED TO *MAKE* THE TIME.

Get up at 5 a.m.

Switch off social media.

Take a career break.

Stop watching television.

Meditate. It will make you feel like you've got more time.

12. Multiple passions

Have you ever felt like there was something wrong because you're not consumed by one single, clear passion in your life? You're certainly not alone.

The people who have clarity about a single career path or a sole passion are fewer than you think. Those who begin with a solitary focus often find themselves bored down the line, so it makes good sense to pursue multiple interests and passions rather than narrowing your attention to one.

Some examples

> If you love photography, cooking, and nature, start a small business taking people on foodie tours and teaching them photographic skills.

> If you're into writing, helping people, and design, create your own beautiful blog and share your ideas about how to change people's lives.

> If you're passionate about caring for the environment, supporting refugees, and social media, offer your services as social media manager to an organization that does work in a field you care about.

What about you? Can you find a way to bring your multiple passions and interests together?

> List all of your various passions, skills, and strengths and think about how you can roll these into potential jobs, careers, or hobbies.

> It's not the easiest thing to do, but stick with it for at least a few weeks and if you feel stuck, consider brainstorming ideas with a couple of creative friends.

They have multiple passions too . . .

TAVI GEVINSON is a fashion blogger, founder, and editor-in-chief of a magazine that focuses on issues impacting teenage girls. She's also an actor and a women's rights activist.

PATTI SMITH has a passion for poetry, literature, music, photography, and activism, and has also tried her hand at acting.

KRISTA TIPPETT studied theology and worked as a journalist and political assistant in West Berlin before launching her radio show, *On Being*, where she conducts interviews about the spiritual and moral aspects of human life.

ELLEN DEGENERES is a comedian, television host, actor, writer, producer, and animal rights and LGBT activist. She is also the founder of the lifestyle brand ED by Ellen.

CHERYL STRAYED worked as a waitress, youth advocate, political organizer, temporary office employee, and emergency medical technician before becoming a *New York Times* bestselling author.

VIOLA DAVIS is an actor and author as well as philanthropist and activist in multiple arenas. She has supported public library and school theater programs and is a passionate advocate for the elimination of childhood hunger.

13. Change the way you think

Author and psychotherapist, Russ Harris (author of The Happiness Trap *and* The Reality Slap) *tells us that the brain is strongly biased toward negative thought.*

The average person has many more negative thoughts per day than positive ones, and often those negative thoughts are repetitive. If you want to change your self-belief and become a person who is confident enough to do what you love, start by changing the way you think.

Negative thinking begets negative consequences. It affects your energy levels, colors what you say, influences your actions, and plays a significant part in the quality of your personal relationships. Negative thinking is insidious and invasive, so if it's an issue for you, work hard to change it. Try to catch your repetitive thoughts. You'll most likely discover that you're wasting a lot of energy going in circles inside your mind.

Being with your thoughts

Keep a notebook with you for a week. Every time you catch yourself thinking a negative thought, write it down.

Try meditating for five minutes each morning for a week. Sit in a comfortable chair, focus your attention on your breath, and then "watch" your thoughts in an open way.

WHEN YOU'RE AWARE OF A NEGATIVE PATTERN OF THINKING, DON'T TRY TO FORCE THE THOUGHTS AWAY, JUST START BY BEING AWARE AND CURIOUS.

Practice these exercises and you'll become aware of how frequently you slip into negative, repetitive (and unhelpful) thinking. Over time you'll learn to catch your negative thoughts as you're having them, which gives you a chance to pause before doing what psychologists call "catastrophizing."

Change the way you think

You'll notice that often you make negative thinking worse by judging yourself harshly.

"I shouldn't be having this thought."

"I need to snap out of it."

"I'm hopeless."

Understanding that it's completely natural for the brain to have a negative bias allows you to be more accepting of yourself and inhibits anxiety.

Once you're familiar with your thoughts, try these exercises to help change the way you think.

1. SOFTEN YOUR TONE

Rather than thinking to yourself, "I hate this job," try to think about it in terms that make you feel more empowered. "This isn't the best job, but it will do until I find the right one."

2. CHOOSE A THOUGHT THAT REFRAMES THE NEGATIVE ONE

"I'm not smart enough." Change it to, "I'm resourceful."

"Things are going to go wrong." Change that to, "I can deal with whatever happens."

"They don't like me." Well, actually, "They're not my people."

3. GET SOME PERSPECTIVE

Imagine putting yourself in the center of the frame on your camera and zooming out until you get your whole house, neighborhood, country, and planet in the frame. Zoom out as far as you need to and ask yourself this: In the scheme of things, is it really worth stressing about at all?

14. Peak experiences

You know those moments when everything seems to slow down and you find yourself suddenly, perfectly, and rapturously in sync with the world and what you are doing? They're called "peak experiences." How great would it feel to tap into that bliss on demand?

Peak experiences occur when we're truly connected to what we're doing. People have them in nature, when they're making art, when they're having a meaningful conversation, or in a flash of pure clarity of insight or deep thought.

These moments stand out from everyday experiences and can sometimes be life-changing. They shape how we think of ourselves and often act as guideposts in the choices we make about the future. They often help connect us with the things we love. Often people describe such moments as simple, uncomplicated experiences. They occur when we're fully present in what we're doing.

REMEMBER YOUR PEAK EXPERIENCES.

Make a point of capturing peak experiences so you can reflect on the impact they've had on your life.

What was happening?

_____

Where were you?

_____

Who were you with?

_____

What time of day was it?

_____

How did you feel?

_____

Are there any parts of that you can replicate?

_____

15. How do you want to feel?

You probably already know some of the milestones you want to achieve in the next ten years—earn $65k, buy a house, travel to India, run a half marathon, and maybe start a family.

You might even have a rough idea of what you want to be doing for work, but as Danielle LaPorte suggests in her book, *The Desire Map*, have you ever thought about how you want to *feel*?

Many people shoot for the wrong stars because they believe that it's the external things that will make them happy.

It's true that money gives us choices. And new things can make us happy *momentarily*, but genuine fulfillment comes when we feel at peace with who we are, when we're content with the choices we've made, and when we know how to be happy in the here and now.

As well as thinking about your external goals, think about what you're aiming for on the inside.

How do you want to feel?

1. Grab a pencil and a piece of paper (or your journal) and spend ten minutes answering that question. Keep away from words like "successful" or "rich." Instead think about the feelings that being successful or wealthy would bring.

2. Once you've chosen your words, give them a score out of 10 as to how much you're feeling that now (with 10 being the top score).

3. If you need more inspiration, grab a copy of *The Desire Map*.

How do you want to feel?

I want to feel:

Creative	Courageous
Confident	Passionate
Free	Connected
At peace	Loved
Adventurous	Healthy
Generous	Fascinated
Funny	Wise
Inspiring	Understood
Powerful	Empathic

16. Get started now

You could wait until you know everything there is to know about your chosen field or wait until you've completed a master's degree in what interests you —or you could just get out there and start doing whatever it is you want to be doing now.

In his book *Outliers*, Malcolm Gladwell says that one of the secrets to success is getting experience—and lots of it. Specifically, he quotes 10,000 hours as the magic number to mastering a new skill. Given that the average person spends around 2,000 hours a year at work, that's at least five years of "doing" that you need to accumulate to really master your craft, whatever that may be.

Unless it's absolutely essential, don't wait until you have every additional qualification you think you need. Instead, get started now.

17. A Confident Self

Within each of us are different versions of ourselves. In Hal and Sidra Stone's book, Embracing Your Inner Critic, *they claim the most challenging aspect for most of us is the part they call your "Inner Critic."*

You know how it sounds—it's the voice that tells you you're not good enough, that other people are smarter, funnier, and more likely to be successful than you.

Other selves the Stones refer to are the People Pleaser, the Perfectionist, and the Vulnerable Child (who is scared of change and wants to be taken care of). You might also have an Adventurer, a Warrior, a Storyteller, a Dreamer, a Creative Self, and a Wise Confident Self.

If you've lost touch with these aspects of yourself, they're what Nathaniel Branden called your "disowned" selves. They are there but perhaps you need to tune in to them more.

Think about what kind of person you want to be. Do you want to be confident, creative, articulate, decisive, and funny? Make a note of the qualities that will make you the most confident version of yourself you can be and give a name to that part of you. Or just call it your Confident Self.

IMAGINE WHAT YOUR CONFIDENT SELF LOOKS LIKE, AND HOW SHE OR HE WALKS, TALKS, AND BEHAVES IN A CROWDED ROOM.

When you get stuck in old habitual ways of behaving, ask yourself, "What would my Confident Self do?" Then go ahead and do that. If you have to fake it at first, you'll find it gets easier over time.

18. Be more childlike

Can you remember when you were a child (between seven and ten years old)? What were the things that you loved doing? What about when you were a teenager or a young adult?

You might say playing sports or hanging out with friends but think beyond that—what other details can you remember? Did you love being outside? Did you like hanging out with a crowd, in small groups, or on your own? Once you've cast your mind back, dig a little deeper with this exercise.

Think about what you were innately good at when you were a child, a teenager, and as a young adult, and write down what springs to mind. As well as the things you were good at, what did you just love doing? What did you look forward to, what energized you, and what sort of people were you with when you were happiest?

What activities were you drawn to, even if you didn't have a natural talent for them?

Think about the people who fascinated you most, even if you didn't spend time with them.

Think about the smallest details.

Deep down you are still the same person, although your conscious decision-making may have changed a great deal. *What does the list tell you about what you should do more of?*

Did you love

daydreaming	exploring	adventuring
learning	winning	drawing
reading	imagining	teaching
building	problem-solving	nurturing
making	baking	laughing
coloring	fantasy	being
crafting	leading	independent?

19. Stop magnifying your flaws

No one is perfect, but if you feel that other people have fewer imperfections than you, maybe you're magnifying your flaws and blowing your faults out of proportion.

To develop your self-belief, you need a balanced perspective. Your brain leans toward negative thought, and you need to watch for that because whatever you focus on is what you'll do more of.

> Think of yourself as dull and uninteresting in a social setting and you probably will be.

> Spend time worrying about being forgetful and you possibly will be.

> Tell yourself you're terrible at managing money and, you guessed it, you might be.

> Think negatively about yourself and the world, and guess what you'll convey?

Try this approach instead

> Cut yourself some slack. You know that nobody is perfect, so it stands to reason that everyone is *imperfect*. Every now and then, shrug your shoulders and move on.

> If they bug you so much, learn to overcome your flaws. If you genuinely believe you're dull at dinner parties, prepare some stories and get some party chatter going (have a laugh at yourself, everyone responds to that). If your natural waking state is one of negativity, start the day with a walk, jog, swim, or visit to your yoga mat. If you're hopeless with money, find a financial counselor to guide you. If your memory always lets you down, do some brain training. If you tend to lose perspective, learn to meditate to raise your self-awareness and give you a more balanced view of the world.

LEARN TO MAGNIFY YOUR TALENTS INSTEAD BY REMINDING YOURSELF OF THE THINGS YOU'RE NATURALLY GOOD AT.

20. Trust your intuition

If you've started to doubt your ability to make good decisions—which happens to us all—it is time to reconnect with your intuition.

Intuitive thought is your gut instinct. It's not so much a thought process but rather a feeling about what's right or wrong. The intuitive right-brain spends its time sensing what's going on in your environment, while the cognitive left-brain is busy weighing up pros and cons, intellectualizing, and rationalizing.

You might be able to come up with plenty of reasons to accept or reject a job offer. You could talk yourself into signing a lease on a new apartment or convince yourself to go on that second date, but *if it doesn't feel right, don't do it.*

An intuitive doubt can be felt as a funny tingle, a sensation in your stomach, a wave of unpleasantness, or an unexpected thought popping into your head. Watch for those little signs. Ignore them and there's every chance you'll make the wrong decision.

Reconnect with your innate sense of wisdom

IMPROVE YOUR CONNECTION WITH YOUR SENSES

Put on a piece of music you love and just sit and listen. Resist the urge to do the dishes, browse the internet, or check your emails—*really listen for a few minutes*. Be fully present to your sense of hearing and listen to the music like you're experiencing it for the first time. You can do the same with any of your other senses; it's all about really tuning in, which helps with mindfulness and has similar benefits to meditation.

CATCH YOUR DREAMS

Keep a journal beside your bed. Set your alarm ten minutes earlier than usual for the next seven days and jot down anything you remember about your dreams as soon as you wake, even if it's just symbols or fragments. Over time, you'll discover themes. Eventually, you'll find you can interpret your dreams more easily.

GO WITH YOUR HUNCHES

Start tuning in to your hunches and act on them. See what unfolds. Occasionally you'll get it wrong, but more often than not, you'll find that you were right to trust your intuition.

LISTEN TO YOUR INTUITION.

21. Choose a career

Unless you're one of the lucky few who have a clear calling in life, there's every chance you'll fall into a career that won't be quite right for you.

Make it your mission to discover what you actually want. Rather than just scanning job lists, start by uncovering the elements that are important to you in a career and then take a creative approach to exploring your options.

WHAT DO YOU KNOW? It doesn't matter if you're not exactly sure about your ideal role, just start by scribbling down the things you do know. What are the skills and strengths that energize you? Do you want to work in a team or largely alone? What kind of physical space do you imagine yourself working in? What's the ideal location of your work? What are the things that interest you? What kind of lifestyle do you want?

BRAINSTORM 20 CAREER IDEAS. With a friend, come up with at least 20 potential careers (don't stop before you've got 20). Be completely open-minded and as random as you like.

Don't think of it as choosing a career for life—just start by being creative and bold.

BE INQUISITIVE. Find out what other people do for work. Read journals and magazines that you wouldn't usually read, explore books and blogs where people share their stories, go to business events in fields you're curious about, and contact people who have interesting roles and ask them if they can spare the time for a coffee with you.

TRY IT. Spend a week volunteering or doing work experience in a role that's of interest; you'll soon discover if it was an empty promise or something to pursue.

FIFTEEN YEARS AGO THESE CAREERS DIDN'T EVEN EXIST

App Developer	Sustainability Expert
Zumba Instructor	Corporate Social Responsibility Manager
Stand Up Paddle Board Instructor	SEO Expert
Social Media Manager	Digital Strategist
Vertical Garden Designer	Micro Herb Grower

22. Don't compare

The root of insecurity is comparing ourselves to others or, worse still, the public personas that others project. This robs us of self-belief, and the more we do it, the more dissatisfied with our own lives we become.

Understand why you are comparing—is it because you genuinely want what that other person has or are you making comparisons based on a distorted view of reality? We see a filtered version of other people's lives on social media, so we usually compare the worst of ourselves with the best of others.

For the most part you miss other people's failings and flaws, and ironically these are the parts of yourself you spend most of your time focusing on. Remember that everyone has moments of insecurity (even your friends who look exceptionally confident).

Comparisons are a waste of time. If you have a genuine desire to change your life, start doing something about it. If someone inspires you because they're doing something amazing, proactively develop yourself in the same direction.

At the same time, remember to focus on your unique qualities, traits, and strengths, and think about how you can bring those to life. Learn to appreciate the characteristics that make you an individual.

IT'S FAR BETTER TO BE THE
BEST VERSION OF YOURSELF
THAN A SECOND-RATE VERSION
OF SOMEONE ELSE.

23. Where are you at your best?

The right physical environments will help you to be at your most creative, focused, articulate, and productive.

They're the places you're likely to do well at the things you love doing.

We are innately tuned in to our physical spaces in very personal ways. We're affected by light, color, decor, and even the orientation of a room. The general ambience of a room emanates a feeling, and if we listen to our intuition, most of us know when a place feels right.

Listen to your intuition about the energy of different places. Some will be right for quiet study; others will be better to inspire creativity. Trust the feelings you get from a space—they can be enough to tell you if a job is worth taking, an apartment is worth renting, or whether it's the kind of place where you can be at your most creative.

Take the time to make your home and your workspace the kind of places you want them to be.

Experiment

Choose an activity you love or a project you're working on, and set aside a few hours over the next few weeks to test out how it feels to do it in different places.

Claim a corner of one of the rooms in your house and turn it into a space that feels beautiful to you. Add a few photos and gather together any other props or tools you need to do your best work.

Try writing in a local cafe.

Try out a shared creative space in your local area.

Work in your local park for an afternoon.

Borrow a tent and take your project into the wilderness.

24. Too many ideas

Having too many ideas can be as much of a problem as not having any ideas at all.

People feel paralyzed by too much choice. Psychologists say that the ideal number of options to choose from is three. It's overwhelming when you have many more—you know the feeling when you're in a restaurant where the menu is excessively long.

When you've got too many choices and come to make a decision, you're not only motivated by what you might gain but also driven by fear of what you might lose. What if you get it wrong?

If it feels impossible to choose, the choice you make is to do nothing at all. You've heard it before, but it really is a useful maxim to live your life by: It feels better to regret the things you do than the things you don't do. (Plus, we rarely regret making the wrong choice quite as much as we think we will.)

There are no wrong decisions in life. Often there are several possible "right" choices for the big decisions we make.

EVERYTHING YOU DO WILL END UP BECOMING PART OF YOUR STORY, AND OFTEN THE CHOICES THAT AT FIRST APPEAR TO BE THE BIGGEST MISTAKES END UP BEING OUR GREATEST BLESSINGS.

If you're a habitual procrastinator when it comes to choosing, learn to value the time you're wasting as much as you value the decision-making process itself.

Three things to help you choose

Let it go for a week. Put your conscious decision-making on hold to switch off the analytical part of your brain. This gives your creative, intuitive brain a chance to kick in. Pay closer attention to your dreams and listen to your intuition.

Tune in to your body. Join a half-day meditation or yoga workshop to help you become more aware of your physical body.

Give yourself a deadline and just choose.

DID YOU KNOW THAT YOU HAVE
A SECOND BRAIN IN YOUR GUT
CALLED YOUR ENTERIC NERVOUS
SYSTEM THAT IS HOME TO
ANOTHER ONE HUNDRED MILLION
NEURONS? TUNING IN TO YOUR BODY
TUNES YOU IN TO THAT TOO.

25. Try something new

Sometimes it can be hard to work out exactly what it is you love doing. If you're bored or uninspired by the things you usually do, try something new.

Most of us limit ourselves when it comes to trying out a new interest. If we think that we're not creative, we won't join a painting class or pick up a musical instrument. If we're not naturally sporty, we keep away from physical activity—particularly when it involves groups.

Doing something you've never tried before opens different parts of your brain. It can build new neural pathways, literally changing the way you think.

Try something new

1. Choose an interest that fascinates and scares you a little. Put aside your expectations about being able to do it well— just be open to experimenting and building your capacity for courage rather than concerning yourself with mastering a new skill.

2. If you're really worried you'll make a fool of yourself, get some practice at home before enrolling in a class. Whatever interests you, it's likely that you'll find a YouTube video to help get you started.

3. Once you're ready to move beyond the safety of your own living room, look up the courses offered at your nearest community college or public library. Once you're there, remember it's not about mastery as much as it is about discovery.

26. What kind of person do you want to be?

If you want to really believe in yourself, you need to listen to your heart about the kind of person you want to be.

Don't be seduced by the choices that will impress your family, the friends you went to school with, or the people who live next door; think about what is innately and uniquely you. Then be that person.

CONTRARY TO WHAT WE'RE OFTEN TOLD, THERE'S NO SINGLE VERSION OF SUCCESS.

> You might value being creative, having variety at work, having freedom and autonomy, or surrounding yourself with like-minded people.

What kind of person do you want to be?

> Perhaps you enjoy the trappings and stimulation of city life, and you're happy working long hours to make good money so you can buy beautiful things and have incredible vacations.

> Maybe you prefer a quieter life, where you work shorter hours and sacrifice a promotion so you have time to renovate your house and hang out with your partner.

> It might be your thing to live out of town where you can raise your own chickens, grow vegetables, and start your own CSA; maybe you value the community feel of a regional area.

> Or maybe you don't want to be tied to one place because you value adventure, new challenges, and travel.

MORE THAN LIKELY, YOU'LL HAVE YOUR OWN BLEND OF ELEMENTS THAT DEFINE A SUCCESSFUL LIFE FOR YOU.

Write them down and keep them in mind when making life and career choices. It's inevitable that your preferences will change over your lifetime, so check in from time to time and make sure you're not just living a life that will impress others, but that you're proactively choosing what matters to you right now.

27. Make it happen

It's unlikely that your dream role is going to come and find you (as much as you hope it will).

Most people who are in roles that they genuinely love have worked hard for it. If you find yourself talking about taking a different path but you're doing nothing about it, be honest and ask yourself, "Am I hungry enough to make it happen?"

It might not be possible to just show up at your chosen workplace and offer to volunteer, but it's worth thinking about how you can proactively pursue your dream role.

Try these tips

EXTENSIVELY RESEARCH THE INDUSTRY THAT INTERESTS YOU. Find out who's the best in your chosen field or identify people you admire. Send a personalized, handwritten introductory letter expressing your interest in meeting with that person or working for their organization. Deliver it in person. Follow up with a phone call and if there's nothing available now, ask if you can call again in a few months' time.

Make it happen

LEARN HOW TO NETWORK. Ask for introductions where it feels appropriate. Be proactive and even gently persistent. People actually admire perseverance as long as your contact with them is done in a charming, friendly, and respectful way.

FIND YOUR VOICE. If you're in a job that you already love and you're looking to get promoted, don't be afraid to speak up at a meeting or to express your ideas to your manager.

DEMONSTRATE THAT YOU CAN DO IT. Take on extra responsibilities, offer your services as a volunteer, or create a portfolio that demonstrates your skills.

IT'S NOT THE LUCKY PEOPLE
WHO MAKE IT; IT'S THE ONES WHO
DON'T GIVE UP. THE MEEK MIGHT
INHERIT THE EARTH, BUT IT'S THE
COURAGEOUS WHO ARE MAKING THE
MOST OF IT RIGHT NOW.

28. Look on the bright side

When you're being positive, dopamine floods your system, making you happier and turning on all the learning centers in your brain. Positive people are smarter, they do better in their careers, they make more money, have happier relationships, get depressed less often, and are healthier.

Your optimism levels aren't set in stone. If you're a glass-half-empty kind of person, it's not too late to change the way you view the world. In recent years, revolutionary neurological research has discovered that you can actually create new pathways in the brain and train the way you think. So it stands to reason that if you think positive, you will become more positive.

Look on the bright side

Try these

BE GRATEFUL

Before your feet hit the floor each morning, think of three things you're thankful for. They don't have to be big things—you can be grateful for a hot shower, a warm bed, or the latte you'll have later this morning.

SMILE MORE OFTEN

Smiling makes you more attractive to people, it releases a host of positive chemicals that lift your mood, and can ultimately lengthen your life.

EXERCISE

Even fifteen minutes a day makes a difference to body, mind, and soul. Find something you enjoy and schedule it on a regular basis.

REMIND YOURSELF THAT IT'S NOT PERMANENT

View setbacks as temporary and avoid "catastrophizing." Keep perspective when things go wrong.

REMIND YOURSELF IT'S NOT ALL ABOUT YOU

Understand that bad things can happen to good people.
Ask yourself, could you be taking things too personally?

WATCH YOUR LANGUAGE

Positive people use positive language. Catch yourself if you use
phrases like "It's really hard for me" or "I'm useless at this."
Instead choose something less permanent like "It's been
a tough week, but next week will be better" or "I'm not great
at [this], but I am good at [that]."

MEDITATE

Meditation provides perspective and makes everything seem
a bit brighter. Download a guided meditation or two (you'll find
several of mine on the free Insight Timer app), or join a class to
learn the basics and then make it a regular practice.

RANDOM ACTS OF KINDNESS

Doing something for someone else gives you a "helper's high."
Do or say one kind thing every day.

29. Find your tribe

For each of us, finding our people is life-affirming and liberating.

When you find a kindred spirit—a person who speaks the same language, who thinks like you think—you feel like you're not alone.

How will you know when you find your tribe?

When you're with them, you feel at home.

They often have similar interests, but they're not always exactly the same.

They help you to grow.

You can be yourself and feel accepted.

You feel energized, not depleted.

Their company inspires or excites you.

They cheer you on rather than compete with you.

They celebrate your successes with you.

They make you feel understood.

THE EASIEST WAY TO FIND YOUR TRIBE IS TO START DOING THE THINGS YOU LOVE.

JOIN A MEETUP GROUP or take a class; make time to do the things that you love.

REACH OUT. If you meet someone who you think is a kindred spirit, ask them for coffee.

PLAN AN EVENT. People often wait for others to initiate social gatherings. Organize a lunch or a dinner and invite a handful of friends (even if you don't know them that well).

30. Money won't make you happy

People in developing countries are often happier than those in the so-called first world.

When you're simply meeting your basic needs, you feel a sense of accomplishment and contentment at the end of each workday. Beyond that you start setting aspirational goals (a bigger house, another car, a designer handbag), and the further you go from your basic needs, the more the rate of return decreases, at which point you run the risk of becoming perpetually dissatisfied.

"Affluenza" is a relatively recent phenomenon, but it's a growing problem in the developed world. It's basically a term used to describe people who get caught up in a wave of consumerism and eventually discover that being solely focused on material goals creates a void that no amount of money can fill.

It's far better to focus on finding meaningful, creative work and creating a life that you love than it is to just go after the big bucks.

REGARDLESS OF WHETHER YOU MAKE A LITTLE OR A LOT, CHOOSE A LIFESTYLE THAT IS RICH WITH EXPERIENCES AND MEANINGFUL RELATIONSHIPS, NOT JUST POSSESSIONS.

These are the elements that will make your life memorable and ultimately have the biggest impact on your happiness.

31. Accept the imperfections

There are going to be aspects of every job you don't exactly love.

If you work in a creative business with plenty of flexibility, you're likely to find some ambiguity and there may be very few guidelines to follow. In a structured corporate role, procedures and processes could overwhelm you. Start your own yoga school and you'll still have to learn about managing the finances.

Regardless of what job you choose, there are going to be elements you don't like, but if 30 percent of your time is spent doing stuff you're not crazy about, you're doing pretty well.

REMEMBER TO PAY ATTENTION
TO THE PARTS THAT ARE
GOING WELL AND CREATE STRATEGIES
FOR DEALING WITH THE PARTS
THAT CHALLENGE YOU MOST.

Some people find they work best getting unpleasant tasks out of the way early; others prefer to leave them until the last minute. Get to know your personal preferences, and instead of spending hours thinking about how much you loathe a task, make peace with the fact you don't like it and expend the energy on just getting it done.

What aspects do you love?

Score each of the following areas out of 10 and add them together to work out what percentage of your role you love, and what percentage you loathe.

☐ My co-workers

☐ The actual work I do

☐ The company I work for

☐ The field of work I'm in

☐ The working hours

☐ Management

☐ The skills I use

☐ The level of variety in my role

☐ The flexibility

☐ The money

If the balance is tipped in favor of the things you loathe, what are your options?

Can you outsource or delegate tasks?

_____

Can you have a conversation with your boss about modifying your role?

_____

Can you improve a difficult relationship at work?

_____

Do you need to change your attitude?

_____

Do you need to find a similar role working for another company?

_____

Do you need to change jobs completely?

_____

Is it time to start working for yourself?

_____

32. Lighten up

If you enjoy consuming news, you no doubt find that somewhat stimulating. But you should also keep in mind that most media gives you a fairly negative view of the world.

Bad news sells more than good news (just like pessimism tends to be more influential than optimism), but it's important to remind yourself that it's only part of the overall picture, and to seek out a more balanced view of what's happening in the world.

Spend time with people who have a positive outlook on life and proactively search for good news stories. Google "good news stories" and you'll find a number of publications to subscribe to that focus on sending out messages to help you hold on to a sense of lightness about life. Start with *DailyGood* or the *Good News Network*.

Remember, too, that laughter lowers stress hormones, boosts your immune system, and increases positive endorphins. And it makes you feel great. Sometimes smart people get a bit nervous about having fun. They assume that people who goof around are shallow or vacuous and not informed about the serious aspects of life. You can be smart and funny too—a more balanced way of living is to stay abreast of important news but also remember to relax and let your hair down.

START BY SPENDING TIME WITH PEOPLE WHO KNOW HOW TO HAVE FUN. LEARN TO BE SILLY IF YOU HAVE TO.

If you find yourself saying, "I'll have fun when I'm happier," remember it's a chicken-and-egg kind of problem.

Don't wait for fun to come to you; make a point of creating or pursuing things that lift your spirits and get in there and participate. Don't be too picky or uptight, and don't be the person who hangs back and never wants to try anything new. Say yes more often. Take yourself less seriously. Dance on a table or two. Having a laugh will keep the serious parts of life in perspective.

33. Create a routine

Most successful people run their lives with at least some routine. Even those without a regular daily or weekly structure use small rituals to help them stay grounded.

Learn about the habits that help you create a rhythm so that you can be at your best. If you're naturally bright in the mornings, do your most challenging tasks then. If you find yourself creatively inspired after dark, schedule some after-hours work time for creative projects.

Even if you're not completely in charge of your own schedule, organize your out-of-work hours in a way that builds some structure into your days.

Here's how they do it

Most successful people run their lives with at least some routine.

When **HARUKI MURAKAMI** is writing a novel, he starts his day at 4:00 a.m. and works for five to six hours. Each afternoon he runs or swims, reads for a while, and listens to music. He goes to bed at 9:00 p.m. and keeps this routine every day.

MARIA POPOVA, editor of *Brain Pickings*, meditates in the morning and spends some "nonproductive" active time outdoors every day (not listening to podcasts or reading), before returning home to write. She uses her evenings to catch up with friends and explore creatively inspiring activities around New York City.

WINSTON CHURCHILL woke up at the same time every day and had breakfast in bed while reading his mail and the newspapers. He rose mid-morning and bathed, then took a stroll through his garden. The rest of his day was punctuated by rituals involving eating, drinking, working, napping, and conversation.

Create a routine

CHARLES DARWIN began his day with a short walk, ate breakfast alone, and then spent the rest of his day interspersing work with another two walks, reading letters with his wife, and taking an afternoon nap.

ARIANNA HUFFINGTON avoids her phone in the morning. She starts her day with deep breathing, a gratitude practice, and yoga and meditation.

ANNA WINTOUR plays tennis for an hour every day at 5:45 a.m. at New York's Midtown Tennis Club. Her days are filled with meetings that she starts either early or right on time; she aims to keep every meeting under seven minutes.

Map out your ideal day

What time of day do you do your best work, and where? How long can you work before taking a break? Map out your ideal day including everything you'd love to include. If you're trying to pack too much in, strip it back from there.

6:30 a.m. Meditate

7:00 a.m. Yoga

7:30 a.m. Breakfast

8:00 a.m. Shower

9:00 a.m.–12:00 p.m. Creative work
   (take a break every 30 minutes)

12:00 p.m.–1:00 p.m. Lunch

1:00 p.m.–6:00 p.m. Client work

6:00 p.m. Walk the dog

7:00 p.m. Dinner

10:00 p.m. Bed

34. Build your resilience

Have you ever noticed how some people bounce back easily from adversity while others take a minor blow and seem to give up on their dreams completely?

When you hear some criticism or you make a mistake, remember to keep things in perspective. Nothing in life is permanent and every experience you have provides valuable learning. Remind yourself that you've got the strength to pick yourself up and go on.

Here's what resilient people do

GET BACK OUT THERE AS SOON AS YOU CAN

When you've had a blow, get back out there as quickly as you can. Nothing repairs the damage as quickly as facing the same adversity again. Failing is good, as long as it means you're learning and getting closer to success. Develop new skills if you need to so that you achieve a better outcome next time.

BE FLEXIBLE, OPEN, AND CURIOUS
Resilient people aren't rigid. They look for new and different ways to get around problems, and they're not fixed in their ideas about how things need to be done.

FIND A SUPPORT TEAM
Surround yourself with people who can help. Be comfortable to ask for help when you need to.

BE YOUR OWN CHEER SQUAD
Celebrate small successes along the way and talk to yourself kindly when you make a mistake.

LAUGH IT OFF
Resilient people don't take themselves too seriously. They know when and how to use humor to defuse an uncomfortable situation.

35. Look for role models

Who do you admire most? What are the qualities you see in others that you would like to adopt as your own?

It doesn't matter who you choose as your role model, and you don't need to choose a person for all of their characteristics or qualities—just pick the attributes you would like to emulate.

You might choose as a role model someone who has the confidence you'd like to feel or who has exceptional talent in an area you're passionate about.

Try to find as much as you can about their story. Learn about their failures as well as their successes so you keep a sense of perspective as you navigate your own path. Sometimes we look at a successful person and forget that they've probably made plenty of mistakes that are hidden from the public eye, and that each of those mistakes helped them become the person you are impressed with now.

If you find a role model close to home, make a connection with them. Send them an email and ask them out for coffee. If you can't get close, watch them from a distance and identify the actions that set them apart.

Models and their roles

BARACK OBAMA, inspiration to others

GRACE BONNEY, an eye for design and an early adopter

MALALA YOUSAFZAI, courage and activism

CATE BLANCHETT, grace under pressure

ROGER FEDERER, drive and humility

BRENÉ BROWN, authenticity and the willingness to be vulnerable

ALAIN DE BOTTON, modern philosopher and thought leader

SETH GODIN, clever ideas and pushing boundaries

JANE GOODALL, bravery and commitment to animal welfare

MAYA ANGELOU, creativity, wisdom, humor, and warmth

36. What are you putting out there?

Science has yet to prove that there's any truth in the "law of attraction" theory, but most people will tell you that when they're going through a bad patch or in a grumpy frame of mind, everything seems to spiral.

Equally, when you're doing well, things fall into place. You know the feeling if you've had a stretch of time without a partner. When you finally meet someone and you're in the flush of new love, suddenly you're inundated with attention.

Take some time to think about the energy you're exuding at work, with your friends or in some other area of your life. Are you positive to be around or a bit of a drain?

There are well-documented links between negativity and misery, just as there are between positivity and popularity. Most of us want to avoid the whiner at work, but we'll go out of our way to help someone who's fun to be around.

Who do you want to be?

Try these tips

Give up gossiping for good.

Commit to "no complaints" for a week.

Smile more often.

Send a positive email or say something nice every day for a week.

Stop judging yourself and others.

37. Be bold

For a long time, people believed that nobody could run a mile in less than four minutes.

In the 1940s, the record sat at 4:01 minutes for nine years, and it was assumed that maybe the human limit had been reached. And then in 1954, Roger Bannister did what many considered impossible. He ran a mile in 3:59.4 minutes. Less than a year later someone else ran a similar time, and not long after another three did the same. The current record is 3:43.13, set by Moroccan Hicham El Guerrouj.

What do these athletes have in common? They refused to accept that the limit had been reached. They were bold. They had the audacity to set big goals and then do whatever it took to achieve them. These days, it might be called "changing paradigms" in the workplace. It's basically the belief that the best way to do anything hasn't been discovered yet.

How can you be more bold?

38. Small pleasures

Most of us overestimate how happy we'll be when we change something significant in our lives.

Whether you get a place at a prestigious college, finish your degree, achieve a promotion, get married, or win an important award, the high you'll feel will last no longer than a couple of weeks. Then you're back to your usual level of contentment.

Your external world accounts for just a portion of your long-term happiness. The lens through which you view the world is what makes all the difference.

People say, "I'll be happy when . . . "

> I'm earning $100k.

> I'm 10 pounds lighter.

> I have a house with two bathrooms.

> I've made it to general manager.

> I've met the man of my dreams.

Small pleasures

For most of us, there's no magic "destination" that will make us happy. Successful people usually set new milestones as soon as they reach their goals and spend little time savoring achievements. This can leave us with a perpetual sense of dissatisfaction.

Positive Psychology research tells us that one of the easiest ways to counteract a cycle of dissatisfaction is to learn to enjoy every day. Appreciate small pleasures and proactively . intersperse them throughout your week.

How to be happy now

GET ENOUGH SLEEP. You can cope with everything better after a decent night's sleep.

CREATE A GREAT MORNING. Wake up early enough to go for a walk, meditate, or do some yoga. Eat a decent breakfast, get ready in a leisurely manner, and avoid email before you get to work.

MOVE CLOSER TO WORK. The research says that a shorter commute has a more significant impact on your happiness than buying a bigger house or finding a better job.

DO THE THINGS YOU LOVE. At least once every week, set aside an hour or more to do something you really love doing.

SAVOR EXPERIENCES. Slow down for long enough to really taste what you're eating or to literally smell the roses.

GET OUTSIDE. Spending just twenty minutes outdoors improves your mood and has a positive impact on your ability to think.

SMILE MORE OFTEN. Even a fake smile can boost your mood, but research says that even better are the genuine smiles that crease your eye muscles. Apparently they're the ones that have the most positive impact on your brain.

SPEND TIME WITH PEOPLE WHO MAKE YOU HAPPY. Regardless of how busy you are, make time to connect with the people who make you feel good about yourself.

39. Slow it down

If you want to become more self-aware and more creative, take regular breaks from your phone and whatever other screen you've got used to constantly checking.

We all need time to reflect, to daydream, to make sense of life without constant distraction. While our electronic gadgets make life interesting in so many ways, they limit our capacity for concentration and inhibit our ability to problem-solve and recall information. Social media makes many of us anxious, and flicking between text messages, email, and Google takes us away from real-world relationships.

Being online can fuel your imagination, but you also need time offline to allow new ideas to take shape in your mind in your own unique way. Let technology complement your life, not take it over.

Set some boundaries around time online

Give yourself an hour at the beginning of the day without checking social media and email.

Have one "disconnected" day each week.

Rediscover daydreaming or listening to music without Wi-Fi.

Get out into the natural world and leave your phone at home.

Reconnect with friends without the distraction of a device.

---

40. Don't procrastinate

Most of us procrastinate when we have an unpleasant task to complete or when we're overwhelmed by a huge project.

Sometimes we just do it because we feel unmotivated or disorganized, but at other times it's a way of avoiding pressure or unconsciously sabotaging your success. Review your current goals and ask yourself if the tasks align with your true values. If you discover that they do and you're still sitting on your hands instead of making things hapen, here are some tips to get you moving.

1. CHOOSE ONE THING

Stop overthinking it. Choose one thing to do right now and spend the next five minutes doing that. Make a phone call, write an email—just get started.

2. BREAK IT DOWN

Try mind mapping your idea into manageable steps—it's more interesting than writing a list. Originally developed by Tony Buzan, mind mapping is a simple technique where you begin by writing the project name in the middle of a big sheet of paper, grab some colored markers, and create a series of branches off the central theme with small action steps. Do one of them today.

3. ELIMINATE DISTRACTIONS

Close Instagram and Facebook, turn off your email, and quit any other applications that aren't relevant to what you're working on. Put your phone on silent, and focus on what you're supposed to be doing.

Don't procrastinate

4. SET A REWARD

Tell yourself you'll do the thing that needs to be done for at least fifteen minutes before grabbing your morning coffee or heading out to do something more enjoyable.

5. BE ACCOUNTABLE

If you really can't get started on your own, tell someone else what you plan to get done and set a deadline.
Choose someone who won't easily let you off the hook.

41. Create new habits

You know that exercising at 6:00 a.m. is a great way to begin your day, but some mornings it feels impossible to get out of bed, so you switch off the alarm and go back to sleep. Usually, you spend the rest of the day wishing you'd just done it.

According to US researcher Roy Baumeister, self-control is one of the highest predictors of a happy and successful life. Individuals with high levels of self-control have healthier eating patterns, fewer substance abuse issues, and better financial habits.

Developing self-discipline is a bit like building a muscle— if you begin by focusing on small tasks you can work toward building up to more difficult ones.

Create new habits

Take a look at a few different areas of your life—the way you eat, whether you're getting enough exercise, your work habits, or maybe your living environment.

WHAT ARE YOU DOING WELL, AND WHERE CAN YOU DO BETTER?

Contrary to popular belief, new habits take longer than twenty-one days to create. For most people, it can be anything up to a year to lock in permanent change. If you remember that creating new habits is like flexing a muscle, you can just start by making one small change, and after that you'll find it easier to make another.

Stanford lecturer Dr. BJ Fogg developed a method called "Tiny Habits" to help people create new behaviors. He suggests you start by choosing just one new habit you want to change and spend less than thirty seconds a day on that task. Try doing it at the same time each day and if you can, tack it on to an existing habit you already have. (e.g., flossing just one tooth after you've brushed your teeth). Congratulate yourself each time you do it and stick with it for a week or two to see if you can create a natural new habit.

42. Stop self-sabotaging

If you know what you want but you're dragging your heels, maybe you're sabotaging your own success. Are you setting yourself up to fail?

People self-sabotage for a range of reasons, some of which might be instinctive or deeply buried in their psyche. Common ways to self-sabotage include worrying about what other people will think and focusing on a fear of failure or fear of success.

COMMON WAYS TO SELF-SABOTAGE

> Procrastinating

> Overcommitting

> Blaming

> Being indecisive

> Overthinking

> Pleasing other people

> Comparing yourself to others

> Making excuses

> Having unrealistic expectations

Try this

To stop self-sabotaging, first you have to become aware of it.
Try to catch yourself when you're behaving habitually—even
just saying to yourself, "I'm self-sabotaging," can help, because
the behavior is no longer unconscious. Once you have the
awareness, pause for a couple of minutes and think about a
better option. Keep this up for a few months and you'll create
new ways of being competent.

It might help to remember "the four stages of competence,"
a theory developed in 1970s by the Gordon Training Institute.
It describes the phases we all go through to learn a new skill.

UNCONSCIOUS INCOMPETENCE
CONSCIOUS INCOMPETENCE

—

CONSCIOUS COMPETENCE
UNCONSCIOUS COMPETENCE

43. Everyone starts at zero

If you don't make progress as quickly as you'd like, remember that you're not the only one who's had to struggle.

Most overnight successes didn't actually happen overnight. There's a huge amount that occurs behind the scenes that most of us never see. Success takes time and effort and it comes in all different shapes and sizes—it's not just the size of your audience or your bank account that matters.

When you feel burnt out or dejected, remember why you're doing what you're doing. Keep the picture of your dream alive in your mind. Go at your own pace, but remember that every little action step counts. The most important thing is to just keep at it.

Did you know?

J. K. ROWLING was rejected by twelve publishers before eventually being signed.

BEYONCÉ KNOWLES was voted off a talent show before she became a Grammy Award–winning performer.

VERA WANG failed to make the U.S. Olympic figure skating team. She was later overlooked for the editor-in-chief position at *Vogue* magazine before starting her own fashion label at age forty.

After dropping out of college and launching Apple with his partner Steve Wozniak, **STEVE JOBS** was fired from his own business. He didn't return until over a decade later.

YVON CHOUINARD, founder of Patagonia, started rock climbing at the age of fourteen. Within a few years, he was teaching himself to blacksmith so he could make his own hard-iron pitons. His first shop was in the backyard of his parents' home in California.

ROSARIO DAWSON lived in a squat with her family before being "discovered" on her front porch at the age of fifteen. She has since become an actress, producer, singer, comic book writer, and political activist.

BILL GATES's first software business was a flop.

WALT DISNEY was fired by a newspaper editor because he "lacked imagination and had no good ideas."

URSULA BURNS was raised by a single mother in a low-income housing project in New York's Lower East Side. She went on to become the first black woman to be the CEO of a Fortune 500 company.

44. Develop empathy

Whatever your dream job or life, relationship building is probably the most important skill to develop. And to build great relationships, you must learn to put yourself in other people's shoes.

These days emotional and social intelligence are considered just as valuable as IQ, and most people agree that to do well in life you need a mix of all three.

Empathy is one of the most important elements of emotional intelligence. It begins with being prepared to listen and become aware of other people's feelings, and ends with a feeling of understanding and compassion toward them.

Try these

As soon as you find yourself thinking that you're right and another person is wrong, ask questions to find out why they hold the opinion they do.

Stay open-minded. Often you can learn something if you're open to taking a different point of view.

Let go of having to be right. Relationships matter more. Sometimes it just isn't important—learn to let it go.

Agree (even if you don't). Take the other person's side for ten minutes and think about how you'd argue on their behalf.

You'll have happier relationships and you'll be a much better manager or business owner if you learn the art of empathy.

45. Exercise to boost your confidence

Fast-track your way to stronger self-belief by establishing a regular exercise routine.

The very act of turning up to regular sessions will boost your confidence. Following through on a commitment tells you something about yourself: That you have what it takes to stay motivated and focused on your goals and that you value yourself enough to do the things that are good for you.

EXERCISE

> Makes you smarter
> Releases positive endorphins
> Makes you stronger
> Reduces stress
> Makes you feel more attractive
> Increases immune function
> Improves your mood

Getting started

1. CHOOSE A FORM OF EXERCISE THAT YOU ENJOY.
Find something you're happy to do. If you're into hard-core workouts, a personal trainer might help. If you prefer something gentle, start with a yoga class. If you work in an office all day and need time outdoors, make time for a twenty-minute walk.

2. MAKE IT ROUTINE.
People who keep up a regular exercise habit say that it's essential to establish a routine. Choose your days and times and lock them into your diary.

3. GO WITH A FRIEND.
Nothing is better for keeping you accountable than exercising with someone else. Make a pact that neither of you will pull out.

4. STICK WITH IT.
If you miss a day (or a week), don't let it be an excuse to give up. Get back on the bike—literally.

46. Step out of your comfort zone

Don't wait until you're feeling more confident before you try something new.

Self-belief is a by-product of behavior, so if you're not feeling confident, try mixing things up and try something new. Don't wait until you feel completely sure of yourself, or it will probably never happen.

Doing familiar things cultivates familiar feelings. Doing things that are a little bit challenging grows your confidence.

If the idea of stepping outside your comfort zone terrifies you, start by visualizing yourself doing something different. Imagining an experience actually impacts the brain in the same way as participating in that experience—both activate the same neural pathways.

1. CHOOSE AN ACTIVITY THAT WILL PUSH YOUR LIMITS.

Join an online dating service.

_____

Take a solo vacation.

_____

Make a speech at a
friend's wedding.

_____

Start a blog.

_____

Go out to dinner on
your own.

_____

Approach a prospective
employer.

_____

Book a tandem sky dive.

_____

2. VISUALIZE.

Set aside five minutes every day to close your eyes and
imagine yourself participating in the new activity. Create a mini
TV commercial in your mind and imagine every step of the
process. For example, if you're getting back into dating, create
a picture in your mind where you see yourself walking into a
cafe and confidently greeting a stranger. Imagine how you carry
yourself, see yourself smiling and chatting in a relaxed way.

3. DO IT.

Set a deadline, choose an action step that is measurable in
some way (e.g., organize a date within the next week) and do it.
No excuses.

47. Leave your ego at the door

Don't confuse your ego with self-belief. When you're caught up in ego you want to be right; you need to win against others and your focus is external.

Our egos often cover up our insecurities. If you find yourself being defensive, you're operating from your ego. If you feel superior or compare yourself to others, that's your ego too. If you feel the need to put other people down or gossip about them unkindly, you're operating from ego.

Genuine self-belief is the opposite of ego. It starts with having an inherent understanding of your unique values and your strengths. It means knowing why you make the choices you make.

Self-belief involves understanding yourself well and cutting yourself some slack (and not being defensive) when you make a mistake.

People who believe in themselves deeply don't need to be right and they don't need to make others wrong. They don't judge people harshly and they go easy on themselves. They can listen to criticism objectively and discern those parts that are useful to take on board.

Be mindful of your behavior this week. Pay attention to when you're operating from your ego and ask yourself, "Is there another way to approach this?"

Ego	Self-belief
Feeling superior or inferior.	Feeling good enough.
Being defensive.	Feeling equal.
Criticizing and judging others.	Accepting opinions that differ from your own.
Wanting to intimidate others.	Celebrating others' successes without resentment.
Wanting to be the center of attention (always).	Not needing external validation to feel successful.
Getting upset when people don't agree.	Feeling centred in your values and beliefs.

48. Invite criticism

If you really want to grow, don't just surround yourself with people who support you or are sycophantic. Seek out those who are brave enough to tell you how you can improve.

Try these tips

ASK FOR FEEDBACK. Let people know you're seeking honest feedback—not just praise. Be open to input from everyone you value, and not just those who appear to be ahead of you in life. Sometimes the most brilliant ideas and insights come from the most unexpected sources.

BE CURIOUS. Listen to someone with a completely different perspective to yours. Rather than closing your mind to their point of view, be curious. Find out why they believe what they do.

LISTEN WELL. Don't be defensive.

TRUST YOUR INSTINCTS. It's important to be open and curious, but also smart enough to discard the ideas that don't resonate or don't feel like a good fit for you.

BE SELECTIVE. You don't need to listen to everyone. Some people like to shoot their mouths off without giving much thought to what they're saying. They're not the ones to listen to.

BE DISCERNING. Ask yourself what part of that criticism is useful (if any). Write down the key points in your own words.

RESPOND CALMLY. If you don't agree, don't be defensive. Say, "Thank you, that's interesting."

49. Do it like they do

You've heard the expression "Fake it until you make it."

It can sometimes be a helpful modus operandi for life. Our brains don't differentiate between what we imagine and what we actually do, so even visualizing yourself walking into a room with confidence tells your brain you're more confident.

Observe the way successful people act and behave, and imagine yourself modeling their behavior. Once you've mastered the art of visualizing behavior, give it a try for real. Just make sure you make the necessary modifications to keep it authentic!

Try these

LISTEN like Bill Clinton listens. He makes people feel like they are the only person in the room.

CHARM people like Bono does. He's opened more doors than most politicians.

DRESS like Zadie Smith does. She's sophisticated, original, and unafraid to embrace her own sense of style.

MAKE PEOPLE LAUGH like Hannah Gadsby does. Use humor that is witty, generous, and life-affirming.

TELL GREAT STORIES like Ira Glass does. He makes everyday anecdotes engaging.

DO BUSINESS like Oprah does. She's savvy and entrepreneurial but she's also generous and fun, and loves surprising people.

BE HUMBLE like Martin Luther King was.

50. Your dream matters

When other people don't believe in your dream or when you're not getting traction, it's easy to feel like throwing it in. If you're feeling deflated or uninspired, take a minute to remember how you felt when you were first inspired to follow your heart. Why did it matter to you then?

If those reasons are still valid, and instinctively you sense that your dream is still right for you (no matter what other people say), close your mind to the detractors and critics and just get on with it.

Take stock of what you've already achieved and take a fresh look at the resources at your disposal. If you're feeling overwhelmed, remember you don't need to see the whole staircase, you only need to see the step that's right in front of you.

Break down your big goals into small, manageable steps and focus on the specific things you can do in the next few weeks. Remind yourself that following your dream will make you feel more like the real version of you, and by being true to yourself, you may well inspire someone else to do what they love.

EQUALLY THOUGH, IF IT NO LONGER FEELS RIGHT, IT'S OKAY TO WALK AWAY—JUST MAKE SURE YOU FIND YOURSELF A NEW DREAM.

About
Kate James

Kate James is a coach,
mindfulness teacher,
speaker, and writer.

Through her business,
Total Balance, Kate helps
her clients find their
direction and build
self-belief.

She is a popular
teacher on the
free Insight Timer
meditation app
and the author of
four bestselling
books.

 @total_balance

 @totalbalancegroup

Acknowledgments

With special thanks to the wonderful efforts of Melissa Rhodes Zahorsky, Julie Barnes, and Pip Compton, who have worked collaboratively across the globe to create this beautiful edition of my first book.

Thank you also to the extended team at Andrews McMeel, including Kirsty Melville, Dave Shaw, and Tamara Haus, for giving me the opportunity to publish in the United States and for making the experience so seamless and enjoyable.

Thanks also to Affirm Press for helping me to fulfill my lifelong dream of becoming a published author all those years ago.

And as always, a big thank you to my family—Chris, Elsa, Meg, Toby, Ed, and Oscar—for helping me to believe in myself and for supporting me every day so I can do what I love.

Believe in Yourself and Do What You Love

Andrews McMeel Publishing
a division of Andrews McMeel Universal
1130 Walnut Street, Kansas City, Missouri 64106

www.andrewsmcmeel.com

19 20 21 22 23 SDB 10 9 8 7 6 5 4 3 2

ISBN: 978-1-5248-5090-6

Library of Congress Control Number: 2019931778

Believe in Yourself and Do What You Love was first published
in Australia in 2015 by Affirm Press.

Editor: Melissa Zahorsky
Art Director/Designer: Julie Barnes
Production Editor: Dave Shaw
Production Manager: Tamara Haus

ATTENTION: SCHOOLS AND BUSINESSES
Andrews McMeel books are available at quantity discounts with
bulk purchase for educational, business, or sales promotional use.
For information, please e-mail the Andrews McMeel Publishing
Special Sales Department: specialsales@amuniversal.com.